T0055981

Bob Chilcott
Carols 2

10 carol arrangements for mixed voices

MUSIC DEPARTMENT

OXFORD
UNIVERSITY PRESS

OXFORD
UNIVERSITY PRESS

Great Clarendon Street, Oxford OX2 6DP, England
198 Madison Avenue, New York, NY 10016, USA

Oxford University Press is a department of the University of Oxford.
It furthers the University's aim of excellence in research, scholarship,
and education by publishing worldwide

Oxford is a registered trade mark of Oxford University Press
in the UK and in certain other countries

© Oxford University Press 2006, 2009

Database right Oxford University Press (maker)

This collection first published as *Gaudete!* 2006
This edition © Oxford University Press 2009

All rights reserved. No part of this publication may be reproduced,
stored in a retrieval system, or transmitted, in any form or by any means,
without the prior permission in writing of Oxford University Press,
or as expressly permitted by law. Enquiries concerning reproduction
outside the scope of the above should be sent to the Music Copyright
Department, Oxford University Press, at the address above

Permission to perform the works in this anthology in public
(except in the course of divine worship) should normally be obtained
from the Performing Right Society Ltd. (PRS), 29/33 Berners Street,
London W1T 3AB, or its affiliated Societies in each country throughout
the world, unless the owner or the occupier of the premises
being used holds a licence from the Society

Permission to make a recording must be obtained in advance
from the Mechanical Copyright Protection Society Ltd. (MCPS),
Elgar House, 41 Streatham High Road, London SW16 1ER,
or its affiliated Societies in each country throughout the world

9 10

ISBN 978-0-19-336507-0

Music origination by Jeanne Roberts
Printed in Great Britain on acid-free paper by
Halstan & Co. Ltd, Amersham, Bucks

Contents

Away in a manger	4
Coventry Carol	8
Gaudete!	16
Il est né, le divin enfant	24
Jesus, Jesus, rest your head	30
Jingle, Bells	37
Still, still, still	49
Sussex Carol	52
We wish you a merry Christmas	60
What child is this?	68

Composer's note

I wrote this set of arrangements towards the end of 2005, and decided to dedicate them to some of the choirs and individuals with whom I have a close association. Three of the pieces are reworkings of arrangements I had written before: 'Il est né' was originally written in 1983 for the vocal group The Light Blues, and 'Away in a manger' was written in 1992 for the King's Singers and the Toronto Symphony Orchestra—in this one the audience always joined in! 'Sussex Carol' was originally written for upper voices for the volume *World Carols for Choirs*. The others are completely new, and the accompanied carols can be performed either with piano, or organ if appropriate, or in their orchestrated versions.

I am very grateful to Jane Griffiths for all her work on this volume.

Orchestral parts for the accompanied carols are available to hire from the publisher.

for Jonathan Rathbone and the Barnet Choral Society

Away in a manger

Anon., 19th cent.

Melody: W. J. Kirkpatrick (1838–1921)
arr. BOB CHILCOTT (b. 1955)

*Alternatively, bars 4–22 can be sung by *tutti* sopranos or *tutti* altos.
Orchestral material is available to hire from the publisher: hp, str

© Oxford University Press 2006

Printed in Great Britain

OXFORD UNIVERSITY PRESS, MUSIC DEPARTMENT, GREAT CLARENDON STREET, OXFORD OX2 6DP

Photocopying this copyright material is ILLEGAL.

*If desired, the audience/congregation may join in with singing the melody from bar 24 until the end.

33
makes. I love thee Lord Je - sus! Look down from the sky, And_
love thee Lord Je - sus! Look down from the sky, And_ stay by my
38
stay by my side un - til morn - ing is nigh.
side un - til morn - ing is nigh.
43
unis. pp
Be near me, Lord Je - sus; I ask thee to stay Close
pp
pp

49
by me for ev - er, and_ love me, I pray. Bless all the dear chil- dren in__
55
thy ten - der care, And_ fit us for hea - ven, to__ live with thee
60
there.
rit.
rit.
pp
ppp

for Simon Halsey and the CBSO Chorus

Coventry Carol

From the Pageant of the
Shearmen and Tailors (15th cent.)

English trad.
arr. BOB CHILCOTT

Orchestral material is available to hire from the publisher: fl, ob, 2cl, bsn, 2hn, str

© Oxford University Press 2006. Photocopying this copyright material is ILLEGAL.

18
mf
mp
-ly, lul - lay, thou lit - tle ti-ny child, By by, lul - ly, lul -
mf
mp
mf
mp
24
p dolce
unis. p
-lay. O sis - ters too, How
p dolce
p dolce
p
mf
30
poco cresc.
mp
div.
This
S.
A.
may we do For to pre - serve this day
poco cresc.
mp

35
poor young - ling, For whom we do sing, By by, lul -
This poor young - ling, For whom we do sing, lul -
mp
mf
mp
40
-ly, lul - lay?
-ly, lul - lay?
Lul-ly, lul - la, thou lit - tle ti - ny
S.
A.
T.
B.
p
p
p
p
46
child, By by, lul - ly, lul - lay, thou lit - tle ti-ny child,
mp dolce
mf
mp dolce
mf
mp dolce
mf

52
mp
p dolce
By by, lul - ly, lul - lay.
mp
p dolce
mp
p dolce
58
T.
B.
unis. f
He-rod, the King, In his rag - ing,
f
62
ff con forza
div.
Charg-èd he hath this day His men of
ff

66
might, In his own sight, All young chil -
70
- dren to slay.
mf dim.
74
S.
A.
p
Lul - ly, lul - la, thou lit - tle ti - ny
T.
B.
p
p

79
mp dolce
mf
child, By by, lul - ly, lul - lay, thou lit - tle ti-ny child,
mp dolce
mf
mp dolce
mf

85
mp
p dolce
By by, lul - ly, lul - lay.
mp
p dolce
mp
p dolce

91
unis.
pp sempre
That woe is me, Poor child for thee! And ev - er
unis.
pp sempre
pp sempre
96
p
morn and day, For thy part - ing Nei-ther say nor sing
p
p
102
pp
By by, lul - ly, lul - lay.
pp
pp

108
div.
pp
p dolce
Lul - ly, lul - la, thou lit - tle ti - ny child, By by, lul - ly, lul -
div.
pp
p dolce
p espress.
mp dolce
114
mp
p
-lay, thou lit - tle ti - ny child, By by, lul - ly, lul -
mp
p
mp
p
120
pp
rit.
- lay.
pp
rit.
pp

for Steve Jones and the City Chamber Choir

Gaudete!

Piae Cantiones, 1582

arr. BOB CHILCOTT

Orchestral material is available to hire from the publisher: fl, ob, 2cl, 2bsn, 2hn, 2tpt, timp, str

© Oxford University Press 2006. Photocopying this copyright material is ILLEGAL.

6
1.
2.
Vir - gi - ne: gau - de - te!
Vir - gi - ne: gau - de - te!
7
mp
S.
A.
Tem-pus ad-est gra-ti-ae, Hoc quod op-ta-ba - mus; Car-mi-na lae-ti-ci-ae
mp
10
f
S.
A.
De-vo-te red-da - mus. Gau - de - te! gau-de-te! Chri-stus est na - tus
T.
B.
f
f

13
Ex Ma - ri - a Vir - gi - ne: gau - de - te!
15
mp
T.
B.
De-us ho-mo fac-tus est, Na-tu-ra mi-ran - te; Mun-dus re-no-va-tus est
mp
18
f
S.
A.
Gau - de - te! gau - de - te!
T.
B.
A Chri-sto reg-nan - te.
f
f

20
Chri-stus est na - tus Ex Ma - ri - a

22
p sempre
Vir - gi - ne: gau-de - te!
E - ze-chie-lis por - ta
p sempre
mp

24
Clau-sa per-tran-si - tur; Un-de Lux est or - ta, Sa-lus in-ve-ni - tur.
27
Gau - de-te! gau - de-te!
Gau - de - te! gau-de-te! Chri-stus est na - tus Ex Ma - ri - a
Gau - de-te! gau - de-te!
Gau - de - te! gau-de-te! Chri-stus est na - tus Ex Ma - ri - a
p sempre

30
f
Vir - gi - ne: gau - de - te!
Er - go nos - tra con - ci - o
f
f

32
Psal - lat iam in lus - tro; Be - ne - di - cat Do - mi - no: Sa - lus Re - gi nos - tro.

35
Gau - de - te! gau - de - te! Chri - stus est na - tus
37
Ex Ma - ri - a Vir - gi - ne: gau - de - te!

39
ff
Gau - de - te! gau - de - te! Chri - stus est na - tus
ff
ff
41
fff
Ex Ma - ri - a Vir - gi - ne: gau - de - te!
fff
fff

for Mark Sirett and the Cantabile Choirs, Kingston, Ontario

Il est né, le divin enfant

French trad.
arr. and trans. BOB CHILCOTT

© Oxford University Press 2006. Photocopying this copyright material is ILLEGAL.

5
-nez mu-set - tes; Il est né, le di-vin en - fant, Chan-tons tous son a-vè - ne-
-loud to greet him; He is born to us on earth, Ce - le - brate the Ho - ly
(loo)
(loo)
(loo)
8
After initial refrain and also vv. 1–3
Fine (after v. 4)
-ment.
Birth.
(loo)
loo loo loo.
(loo)
loo
(loo)
loo
After initial refrain and also vv. 1–3
Fine (after v. 4)

VERSE 1
10
mp
A.
De-puis plus de qua-tre mille ans, Nous le pro-met-taient les pro-phè-tes,
Since for ma-ny a thou-sand year Pro-phets told us of his com-ing,
mp
T.
De-puis plus de qua-tre mille ans, Nous le pro-met-taient les pro-phè-tes,
Since for ma-ny a thou-sand year Pro-phets told us of his com-ing,
mp
div.
B.
loo (etc.)
mp
D.S. 𝄋 Refrain then to v. 2
14
De-puis plus de qua-tre mille ans, Nous at-ten-dions cet heu-reux temps.
Since for ma-ny a thou-sand year, We might see the child ap-pear.
De-puis plus de qua-tre mille ans, Nous at-ten-dions cet heu-reux temps.
Since for ma-ny a thou-sand year, We might see the child ap-pear.
(loo)
D.S. 𝄋 Refrain then to v. 2

VERSE 2
25
div. p legato
S.
loo loo loo loo loo (etc.)
p
A.
Ah! qu'il est beau, qu'il est char-mant, Ah! que ses grâ - ces sont par-fait - es!
He is gen - tle, he is mild, Show-ing us his grace and beau - ty!
p
T.
Ah! qu'il est beau, qu'il est char-mant, Ah! que ses grâ - ces sont par-fait - es!
He is gen - tle, he is mild, Show-ing us his grace and beau - ty!
div. p legato
B.
loo (etc.)
p
p
29
D.S. 𝄋 Refrain then to v. 3
(loo)
Ah! qu'il est beau, qu'il est char-mant, Qu'il est doux, ce di - vin en - fant!
He is gen - tle, he is mild, Born for us, this Ho - ly Child!
Ah! qu'il est beau, qu'il est char-mant, Qu'il est doux, ce di - vin en - fant!
He is gen - tle, he is mild, Born for us, this Ho - ly Child!
(loo)
D.S. 𝄋 Refrain then to v. 3

VERSE 3
40
mp
A.
Une é - ta - ble est son loge - ment, Un peu de paille est sa cou - chet - te;
Ly - ing in an ox - 's stall, On - ly a bed of straw en - folds him,
mp
T.
Une é - ta - ble est son loge - ment, Un peu de paille est sa cou - chet - te;
Ly - ing in an ox - 's stall, On - ly a bed of straw en - folds him,
mp legato
div.
B.
loo (etc.)
mp
D.S. 𝄋 Refrain then to v. 4
44
Une é - ta - ble est son loge - ment, Pour un Dieu quel a - bais - se - ment!
Ly - ing in an ox - 's stall, He is come, the King of all!
Une é - ta - ble est son loge - ment, Pour un Dieu quel a - bais - se - ment!
Ly - ing in an ox - 's stall, He is come, the King of all!
(loo)
D.S. 𝄋 Refrain then to v. 4

VERSE 4
55
div. mf
S.
O Jé - sus, roi tout puis - sant, Si pe - tit en - fant que vous ê - tes;
Je - sus, King, whom we a - dore, As a child you come a - mong us;
mf
A.
O Jé - sus, roi tout puis - sant, Si pe - tit en - fant que vous ê - tes;
Je - sus, King, whom we a - dore, As a child you come a - mong us;
mf
T.
O Jé - sus, roi tout puis - sant, Si pe - tit en - fant que vous ê - tes;
Je - sus, King, whom we a - dore, As a child you come a - mong us;
div. mf legato
B.
loo (etc.)
mf
59
f
dim.
D.S. 𝄋 Refrain to Fine
O Jé - sus, roi tout puis - sant, Ré - gnez sur nous en - tiè - re - ment.
Je - sus, King, whom we a - dore, Reign in glo - ry for ev - er - more.
f
dim.
O Jé - sus, roi tout puis - sant, Ré - gnez sur nous en - tiè - re - ment.
Je - sus, King, whom we a - dore, Reign in glo - ry for ev - er - more.
f
dim.
O Jé - sus, roi tout puis - sant, Ré - gnez sur nous en - tiè - re - ment.
Je - sus, King, whom we a - dore, Reign in glo - ry for ev - er - more.
Ré - gnez sur nous en - tiè - re - ment.
Reign in glo - ry for ev - er - more.
f
dim.
(loo)
loo loo loo
D.S. 𝄋 Refrain to Fine
f
dim.

for David Wordsworth and the Addison Singers

Jesus, Jesus, rest your head

American trad.
arr. BOB CHILCOTT

Orchestral material is available to hire from the publisher: hp, str
© Oxford University Press 2006. Photocopying this copyright material is ILLEGAL.

poco rit.
mp
at their birth,
7
div.
poco cresc.
S.
A.
All the wea - ry folk on earth Sleep in si - lence at their
T.
B.
p poco cresc.
mp
poco rit.
poco cresc.
mp
a tempo
Je-sus, Je-sus, rest your head,
9
p
dolce
birth, rest your head, You have got a man-ger bed.
p
dolce
a tempo
p

12
p
Have you heard a-
unis. mp
Have you heard a - bout our Je- sus,
mp dolce
mp
15
mp
unis.
-bout our Je - sus, How the shep-herds went to the sta - ble
p
div.
Have you heard a - bout his fate? How the shep - herds

17
p
mp
div.
On that Christ-mas Eve so late? Winds are blow-ing, cows are low-ing,
on that Eve so late?
mp
19
p dolce
S.1
Stars are glow-ing, glow-ing, glow-ing, Je-sus, Je-sus, rest your head,
S.2
Stars are glow-ing, glow-ing, glow-ing, Je-sus, Je-sus,
A.
Stars are glow-ing, glow-ing, glow-ing, glow-ing,
T.
Stars are glow-ing, glow-ing, glow-ing, glow-ing,
B.
Stars are glow-ing, glow-ing, glow-ing, glow-ing,
p dolce

21
You have got a man-ger bed.
rest your head, You have got a man-ger bed.
glow - ing.
glow - ing.
glow-ing.
24
SOPRANO SOLO
p dolce
S. SOLO
Je - sus rest your head,
TUTTI
p dolce
S.
Je - sus, Je - sus, rest your head,
p dolce
A.
Je - sus, Je - sus, rest your head,
p dolce
T.
Rest your head,
p dolce
B.
Rest your head,

26
Je - sus rest your head,
poco cresc.
You have got a man-ger bed, All the wea-ry folk on earth
poco cresc.
You have got a man-ger bed, All the wea-ry folk on earth
poco cresc.
man-ger bed, All the wea-ry folk on earth
poco cresc.
man-ger bed, All the wea-ry folk on earth
poco cresc.
29
poco rit.
mp
a tempo
p
S.
Sleep in si-lence at their birth, Je-sus, Je-sus, rest your head,
A.
Sleep in si-lence at their birth, rest your
T.
Sleep in si-lence at their birth, rest your
B.
Sleep in si-lence at their birth, rest your
poco rit.
a tempo
mp
p

31
dolce
You have got a man-ger bed.
dolce
head,
You have got a man-ger bed.
dolce
head,
You have got a man-ger bed.
dolce
head,
You have got a man-ger bed.
mp dolce
poco rit.
slower
rit.
pp
34
S.
A.
Je-sus, Je-sus, rest your head.
Je-sus, Je-sus, rest your head.
T.
B.
Je-sus, rest your head.
pp
poco rit.
slower
rit.
p
pp

for the Amabile Choirs, London, Ontario

Jingle, Bells

Words and melody: J. Pierpont (1822–93)
arr. BOB CHILCOTT

Orchestral material is available to hire from the publisher: 2fl, 2ob, 2cl, 2bsn, 2hn, sleigh bells, glock, hp, str

© Oxford University Press 2006. Photocopying this copyright material is ILLEGAL.

10
mf
div.
p
S.
A.
sleigh - ing song to - night. Oh! Jin - gle, bells, jin - gle, bells,
mp
p
T.
B.
Oh! Jin - gle, jin - gle, bells, jin - gle,
mf
p
12
mp
jin - gle all the way; Oh, what fun it is to ride in a
mp
bells, jin - gle, jin - gle all the way; what fun it is to ride in a
mp

14
sub. p
one-horse o-pen sleigh! Oh! Jin-gle, bells, jin-gle, bells,
sub. p
one-horse o-pen sleigh! Oh! Jin-gle, jin-gle, bells, jin-gle,
sub. p
16
mp
jin-gle all the way; Oh, what fun it is to ride in a one-horse o-pen
mp
bells, jin-gle, jin-gle all the way; what fun it is to ride in a one-horse o-pen
mp

18
mf
sleigh.
mf
Now the ground is
mf
sleigh.
unis. mf
Now the ground is white;
mf
p
mf
21
white;
Go it while you're young,
And sing this
Go it while you're young,
Take the girls to - night,
And

23
unis.
sleigh - ing song. Just get a bob-tailed bay, Two -
sing this sleigh-ing song. Just get a bob-tailed
25
div.
cresc.
-for - ty for his speed; Then hitch him to an o - pen sleigh And
cresc.
bay, Two-for - ty for his speed; an o - pen sleigh And
cresc.

27
f
Jin - gle, bells, jin - gle, bells,
crack! you'll take the lead. Oh! Jin - gle, jin - gle, bells, jin - gle,
f
Jin - gle, jin - gle, bells, jin - gle,
crack! you'll take the lead. Oh! Jin - gle, bells, jin - gle, bells,
f
jin - gle all the way; Oh,
29
bells, jin - gle, jin - gle all the way,
what fun it is to ride in a
bells, jin - gle, jin - gle all the way,
jin - gle all the way; Oh,

31
ff
Jin - gle, bells, jin - gle, bells,
Jin - gle, jin - gle, bells, jin - gle,
one - horse o - pen sleigh! Oh!
ff
Jin - gle, jin - gle, bells, jin - gle,
Jin - gle, bells, jin - gle, bells,
ff
33
jin - gle all the way; Oh,
bells, jin - gle, jin - gle all the way,
what fun it is to ride in a
bells, jin - gle, jin - gle all the way,
jin - gle all the way; Oh,

one-horse o - pen sleigh.
35
one - horse o - pen sleigh. Jin - gle,
one - horse, one-horse o - pen sleigh.
one - horse o - pen, one-horse o - pen sleigh. Jin - gle,
37
p
bells.
p
Dash-ing through the
p
bells.
unis. p
Dash-ing through the snow
In a
p

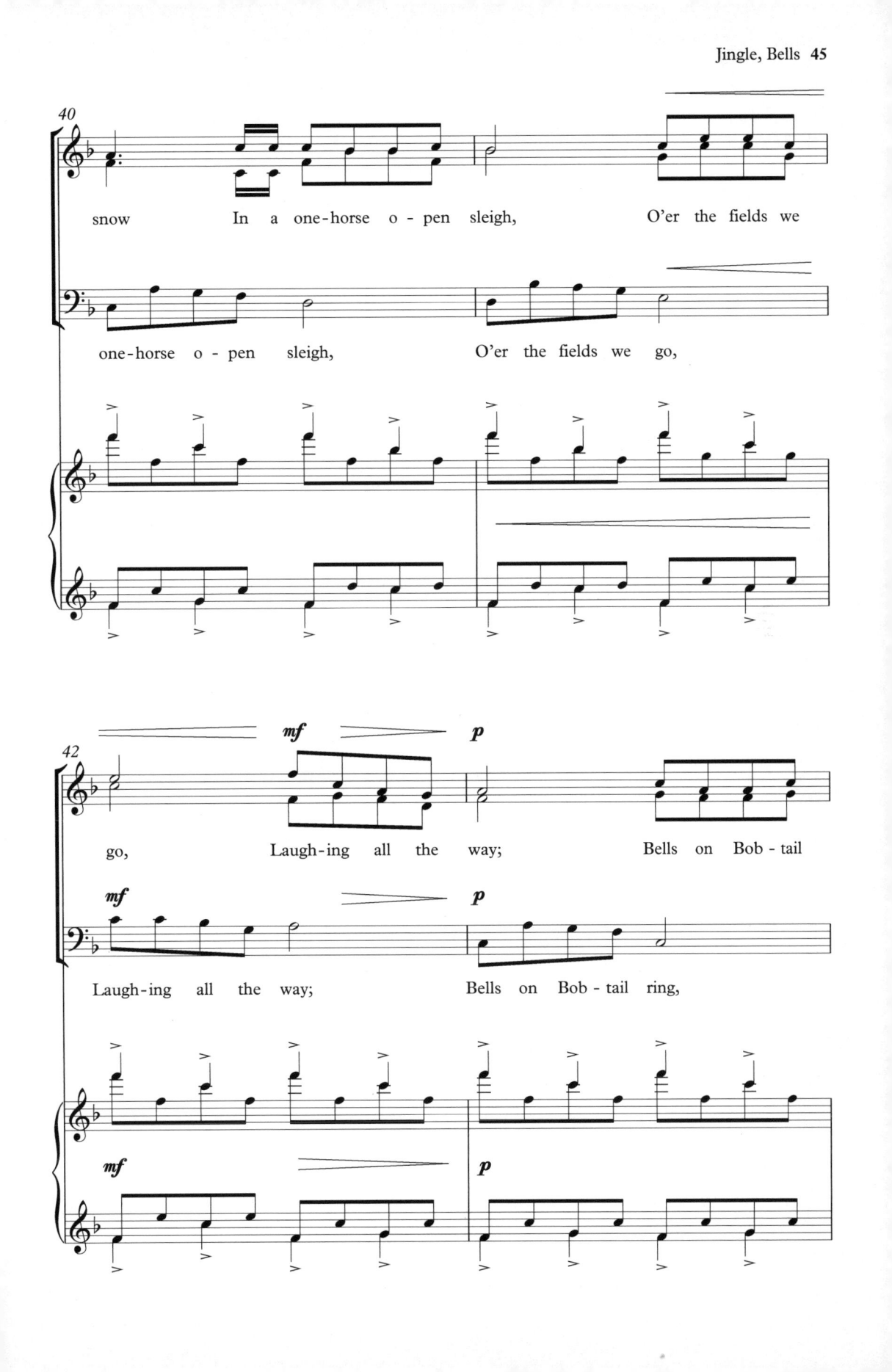
40
snow In a one-horse o - pen sleigh, O'er the fields we
one-horse o - pen sleigh, O'er the fields we go,
mf
p
42
go, Laugh-ing all the way; Bells on Bob - tail
mf
p
Laugh-ing all the way; Bells on Bob - tail ring,
mf
p

44
ring, Mak - ing spi - rits bright; What fun it
Mak - ing spi - rits bright; What fun it is to ride, and sing A
46
mf
sub. p
is to - night. Oh! Jin - gle, bells, jin - gle, bells,
mf
sub. p
div.
sleigh - ing song to - night. Oh! Jin - gle, jin - gle, bells, jin - gle,
mf
sub. p

48
mp
jin - gle all the way; Oh, what fun it is to ride in a
mp
bells, jin - gle, jin - gle all the way; what fun it is to ride in a
mp
50
sub. p
one - horse o - pen sleigh! Oh! Jin - gle, bells, jin - gle, bells,
sub. p
one - horse o - pen sleigh! Oh! Jin - gle, jin - gle, bells, jin - gle,
sub. p

52
mp
jin - gle all the way; Oh, what fun it is to ride in a
mp
bells, jin - gle, jin - gle all the way; what fun it is to ride in a
mp
mf
one - horse o - pen sleigh.
pp
Jin - gle, bells!
54
one - horse o - pen sleigh.
Jin - gle, bells!
mf
one - horse, one-horse o - pen sleigh.
pp
Jin - gle, bells!
one - horse o - pen, one-horse o - pen sleigh. Jin - gle, bells!
mf
pp

for the BBC Singers

Still, still, still

German trad.
arr. and trans. BOB CHILCOTT

© Oxford University Press 2006. Photocopying this copyright material is ILLEGAL.

13
Schlaf,
Sleep,
p
Kind - lein schla - fen will! Still.
child is sleep - ing still! Still.
Schlaf, schlaf,
Sleep, sleep,
Kind - lein schla - fen will! Still.
child is sleep - ing still! Still.
mp
Kind - lein schla - fen will! Still.
child is sleep - ing still! Still.
p
17
schlaf, mein lie - bes Kind - lein schlaf! Die
sleep, my lit - tle ba - by sleep! The
20
En - gel tun schön mu - si - zie - ren, vor dem Kind - lein
ang - els sing and tell the sto - ry of the child who
23
ju - bi - lie - ren. Schlaf, schlaf, schlaf, mein lie - bes Kind - lein
comes in glo - ry. Sleep, sleep, sleep, my lit - tle ba - by

poco rit.
pp
a tempo
mf dolce
schlaf, schlaf!
sleep, sleep!
27
schlaf, schlaf, schlaf, schlaf! Gross, gross, gross, die
sleep, sleep, sleep, sleep! Joy, joy, joy, our
pp
mf dolce
schlaf, schlaf!
sleep, sleep!
31
Lieb ist üb - er - gross! Gott hat den Him - mels -
hearts are filled with joy! The Lord has come from
Lieb ist üb - er - gross!
hearts are filled with joy!
34
-thron ver - las - sen und muss rei - sen auf der Strass - en. Gross, gross,
heaven a - bove us to this world to guide and love us. Joy, joy,
rit.
mp dim.
p
Lieb ist üb - er - gross!
hearts are filled with joy!
38
gross, die Lieb ist üb - er - gross!
joy, our hearts are filled with joy!
mp dim.
p
gross, die Lieb ist üb - er - gross!
joy, our hearts are filled with joy!

for David Lawrence and the City of Birmingham Young Voices

Sussex Carol

English trad.
arr. BOB CHILCOTT

Orchestral material is available to hire from the publisher: 2fl, 2ob, 2cl, 2bsn, 2hn, 2perc (triangle, glock), str

© Oxford University Press 2006. Photocopying this copyright material is ILLEGAL.

7 div. mf
S.
A.
News of great joy, news of great mirth, News of
unis. f
T.
B.
mf
f
mf
f
11
our mer - ci - ful King's birth.
15
unis. f
Then why should men on earth be so sad, Since
unis. f
Then why should men on

19
our Re-deem - er made us glad, Then why should men on
earth be so sad, Since our Re-deem - er made us glad, Then

22
earth be so sad, Since our Re-deem - er made us glad?
why should men on earth be so sad, He made us glad?

25 div. mf
f
unis.
When from our sin he set us free, All for
div.
unis.
mf
f
mf
f
29
to gain our li - ber - ty?
33
SOPRANO f
S.
When sin de - parts be -
unis. f
T.
B.
When

36
S.
- fore_ his grace, Then life and health come in its place, When
A.
f
When sin de - parts be - fore_ his grace, Then
T.
B.
sin de - parts be - fore_ his grace, Then life and health come
39
sin de-parts be - fore_ his grace, Then life and health come
life and health come in its place, When sin de-parts, health
in its place, When sin de-parts be - fore_ his grace, health

42
mf
S.
in its place. Ang - els and men with joy may sing,
A.
in its place. Ang - els and men with joy may sing,
T.
in its place. Ang - els and men with joy may sing,
B.
in its place. Ang - els and men with joy may sing,
mf
unis.
46
f
S.
A.
All for to see the new - born King.
unis.
T.
B.
f
ff

51
S.
ff
All out of dark - ness we_ have light which
A.
ff
All out of dark - ness we have light which
T.
B.
ff
All out of dark - ness we_ have light which
55
1.
2.
made the ang - els sing this night. All sing this night:
made the ang - els sing this night. All sing this night:
made the ang - els sing this night. All sing this night:
1.
2.

57
f
'Glo - ry to God and peace to men,
f
'Glo - ry to God and peace to men,
f
'Glo - ry to God and peace to men,
f
60
unis.
ff
S.
A.
Now and for ev - er - more, A - men.
unis.
T.
B.
ff
ff
64
div.
Now and for ev - er, A - men.'
div.

for Sheila Harrod and the Kentwood Showchoir

We wish you a merry Christmas

Trad. West Country carol
arr. BOB CHILCOTT

Orchestral material is available to hire from the publisher: fl, cl, 2hn, 2tbn, 2perc (drum kit, bongos), str

© Oxford University Press 2006. Photocopying this copyright material is ILLEGAL.

15
you and your kin; We wish you a mer-ry Christ-mas And a
19
ff
hap-py New Year.
ff
ff
f
24
mf
Now bring us fig-gy
unis. f
Now bring us some fig-gy pud-ding, Now bring us some fig-gy

28
pud - ding, And bring some, bring some out
pud - ding, Now bring us some fig - gy pud - ding, And bring some out
32
DESCANT
f
Good tid - ings we bring To___ you and your kin; We
S.
A.
f
here. Good tid - ings we bring To___ you and your kin; We
T.
B.
div.
here.
f
f

37
ff
wish you a mer-ry Christ-mas, And a hap - py New
ff
wish you a mer-ry Christ-mas, And a hap - py New
ff
ff
41
Year.
unis. f
For we all like fig-gy
Year.
mf
For we
f

46
S.
A.
pud - ding, We all like fig - gy pud - ding, For we
T.
B.
all like fig - gy pud - ding,
49
p sub.
all like fig - gy pud - ding, So bring some out here.
Good
So bring some, bring some out here.
p sub.
53 div.
cresc.
tid - ings we bring To you and your kin; We
cresc.
p sub.
cresc.

57
f
wish you a mer-ry Christ-mas And a hap-py New
f
f
61
f
And we
Year.
65
won't go un-til we've got some, We won't go un-til we've got some, And we
mf
won't go, won't go, won't go, won't go,
mf
mf

69
DESC.
DESCANT
ff
Good
won't go un-til we've got some,
S.
A.
ff
won't go,_ won't go, So bring some out here. Good
T.
B.
ff
73
tid - ings we bring To_ you and your kin; We
tid - ings we bring To_ you and your kin; We
ff

77
fff
wish you a mer - ry Christ - mas And a hap - py New
fff
wish you a mer - ry Christ - mas And a hap - py New
fff
81
Year, Hap - py New Year!
Year, Hap - py New Year!
fff

for the Taipei Chamber Singers

What child is this?

English trad.
arr. BOB CHILCOTT

William Chatterton Dix (1837–98)

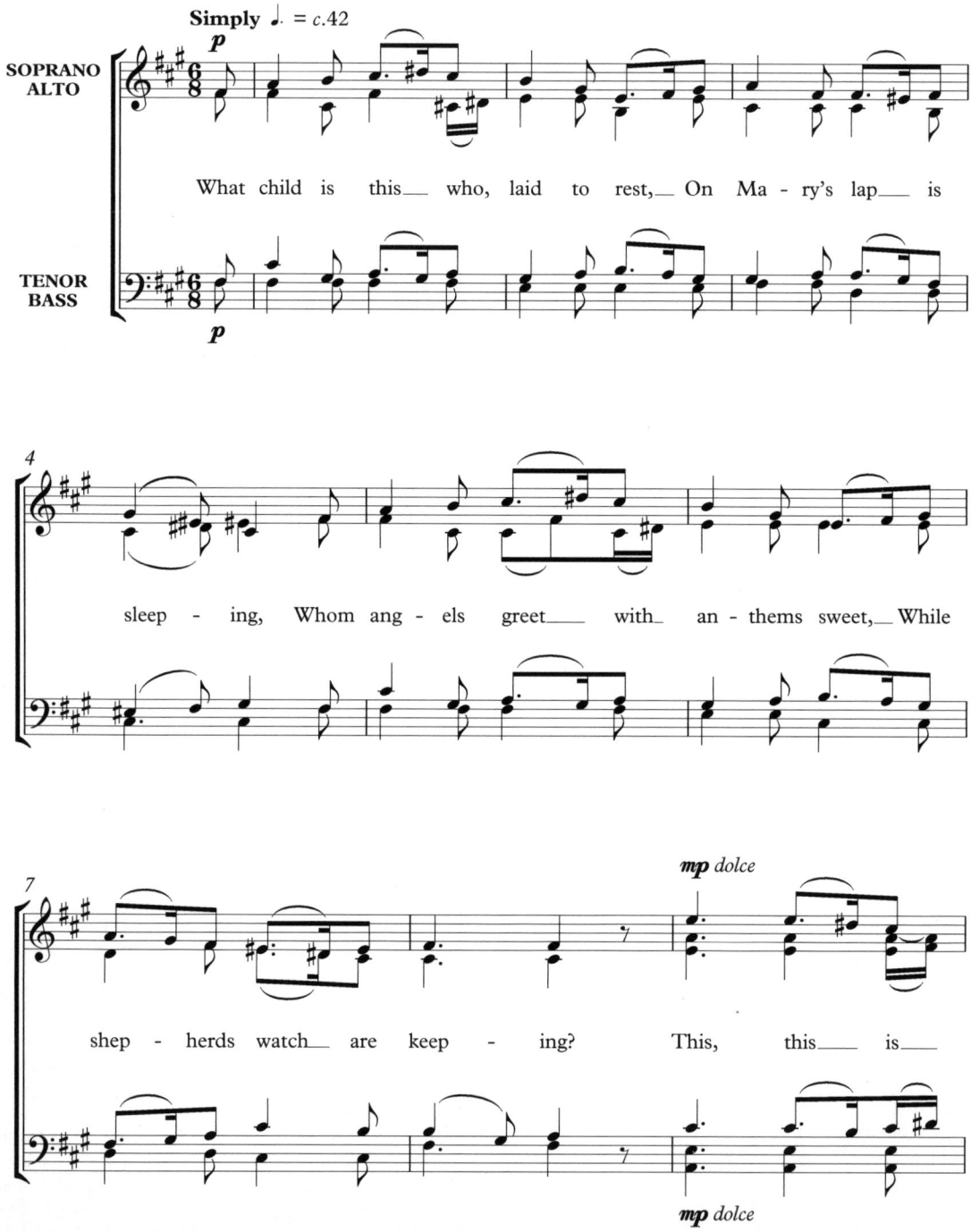

© Oxford University Press 2006. Photocopying this copyright material is ILLEGAL.

10
Christ the King, Whom shep - herds guard and ang - els sing:
13
Haste, haste to bring him praise, The Babe, the Son of
16
mp
Ma - ry.
Why lies he here in such
unis.
mp
Why lies he in such mean es - tate Where
19
mean, mean es - tate?
mean, in such mean es - tate? Good Christ - ians,
ox and ass are feed - ing? Good Christ - ians fear: for

22
fear: The Word is plead - ing.
sin - ners here The si - lent Word is plead - ing.
25
f
Nails, spear shall pierce him through, The cross be borne for
div.
f
28
mf più legato
me, for you; Hail! hail the Word made Flesh, The
mf più legato
31
pp
Babe, the Son of Ma - ry. So bring him in - cense,
pp

34
gold, and myrrh; Come, pea - sant, king, to own him! The
37
King of Kings sal - va - tion brings: Let lov - ing hearts en -
40
mp cresc.
- throne him. Raise, raise the song on high! The
mp cresc.
43
mf
Vir - gin sings her lul - la - by. Joy! joy! for
mf

46
Christ is born, The Babe, the Son of Ma - ry.
49
f
Raise, raise the song on high! The Vir - gin sings her
f
52
mf dim.
lul - la - by. Joy! joy! for Christ is born, The
mf dim.
rit.
55
p
Babe, the Son of Ma - - - ry.
p